LOFTS

Art director: Claudia Martínez
Editorial coordination: Simone Schleifer
Editor and texts: Mariana R. Eguaras Etchetto
Layout: Esperanza Escudero
Translations (English, German, French, Dutch): Equipo de Edición

Editorial project:
2009 © **LOFT Publications**
Via Laietana, 32, 4.º, Of. 92
08003 Barcelona, Spain
Tel.: +34 932 688 088
Fax: +34 932 687 073
loft@loftpublications.com
www.loftpublications.com

ISBN 978-84-92731-01-5   Printed in China

LOFTS

F K G

ts Lofts Lofts Lofts Lofts Lofts Lofts Lofts Lofts Lofts Lofts Lofts Lofts Lofts Lofts Lofts Lofts

Lofts Lofts Lofts Lofts Lofts Lofts Lofts Lofts Lofts Lofts Lofts Lofts Lofts Lofts Lofts Lofts Lofts Lo

hopping Living **Working** Shopping Living Working Shopping **Living** Working **Shopping** Living Working Sh

s Lofts Lofts Lofts Lofts Lofts Lofts Lofts Lofts Lofts Lofts Lofts Lofts Lofts Lofts Lofts Lofts Lofts L

ofts Lofts Lofts Lofts Lofts Lofts Lofts Lofts Lofts Lofts Lofts Lofts Lofts Lofts Lofts Lofts Lofts Lof

Living Working **Shopping** Living Working Shopping Living **Working** Shopping **Living** Working Shopping

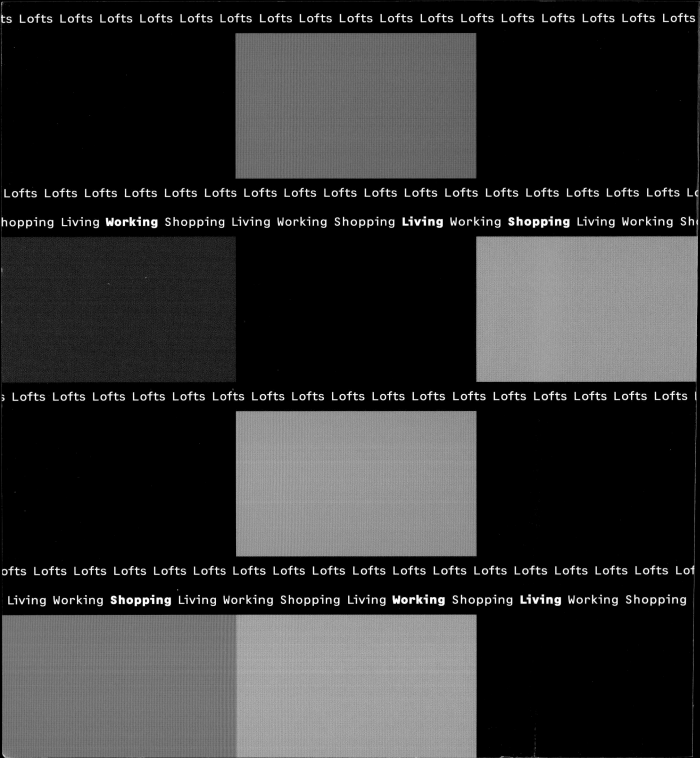

The loft, which originally constituted a type of clandestine life, has become a concept applicable to large, renovated spaces, where the existing structure has been incorporated into everyday architecture.

Consequently, old factories, storage areas and warehouses are being transformed to create homes and offices, or commercial studios and shops. The original architecture of these spaces is characterized by the use of materials such as concrete, aluminum, marble and wood, with smooth walls and large doors and windows.

The decoration in lofts emphasizes simplicity, adaptability and functionality to create open-plan spaces, with separate rooms being formed using folding screens, medium-height walls or simply pieces of furniture.

There are currently two trends: constructing new homes in the style of lofts, and recycling and re-using those already built as a further step in the development of sustainable architecture.

INTRODUCTION

Der Loft, ursprünglich als unkonventionelle, alternative Wohn- und Lebensform entstanden, hat sich in einen Wohnraum verwandelt, der sich vor allem durch seine Großzügigkeit und Alltagstauglichkeit auszeichnet.
Daher werden immer mehr alte Fabriken, Schuppen und Lager in Wohnungen, Büros, Ateliers oder Geschäfte umgewandelt. Die architektonische Struktur dieser Orte ist durch die Verwendung von Materialien wie Beton, Aluminium, Marmor und Holz gekennzeichnet, mit schlicht gestalteten Wänden und dominanten Türen und Fenstern.
In ihrer Einrichtung zeichnen sich *Lofts* durch Einfachheit, Anpassungsfähigkeit und Funktionalität aus, mit dem Ziel, klar strukturierte Orte zu schaffen. Zimmer werden durch Wandschirme, niedrige Mauern oder einfach nur durch Möbel gebildet.
Heute existieren zwei *Loft* -Konzepte nebeneinander: die Errichtung neuer Wohnhäuser, deren Wohnungen an Lofts erinnern, sowie die Nutzung bereits existierender Räume.

EINLEITUNG

À l'origine, les lofts sont d'anciens entrepôts, usines ou ateliers reconvertis en habitation par une population assez marginale, des artistes ou des familles désargentées. D'où une esthétique particulière : de grands espaces sans séparation, et un attachement au passé avec le maintien des éléments architecturaux d'origine (poutrelles métalliques, murs de brique, sols bétonnés…). Une caractéristique qui s'inscrit les lofts dans la recherche actuelle d'une architecture durable.

Aujourd'hui, le terme désigne des logements mais aussi des bureaux ou des boutiques, pourvu qu'ils disposent de vastes espaces, et qu'ils montrent un certain sens de la décoration : volumes dégagés et lumineux, peu ou pas de cloisons, si ce n'est mobiles, une esthétique de la simplicité et de l'épure. À ce titre, le loft peut également se concevoir dans des bâtiments neufs. Désormais, il s'agit donc plutôt d'un art de vivre et de se montrer que d'une stricte nécessité pécuniaire.

INTRODUCTION

De loft, die oorspronkelijk stond voor een vorm van clandestien wonen, is tegenwoordig een woonconcept dat wordt toegepast op een grote, gerenoveerde ruimte waarvan de originele structuur is verwerkt in alledaagse architectuur.

Op deze manier werden oude fabrieken, loodsen en pakhuizen veranderd in woningen, kantoren, studio's en winkels. De originele bouwstijl van deze ruimten zien we vaak terug in het gebruik van materialen als beton, aluminium, marmer en hout, met gladde muren en grote deuren en ramen.

Wat betreft de aankleding kenmerken lofts zich door eenvoud, aanpassingsvermogen en functionaliteit met als doel transparante ruimten te creëren met vertrekken die van elkaar worden gescheiden door middel van panelen, halve muren of het meubilair.

We zien tegenwoordig twee tendensen naast elkaar bestaan: de bouw van nieuwe woningen met de esthetiek van een loft en het hergebruik van bestaande woningen als een nieuwe stap in de ontwikkeling van een duurzame architectuur.

INLEIDING

Lofts Lofts Lofts Lofts Lofts Lofts Lofts Lofts Lofts Lofts Lofts Lofts Lofts Lofts Lofts Lofts Lofts Lo

opping Living **Working** Shopping Living Working Shopping **Living** Working **Shopping** Living Working Sho

Lofts Lofts Lofts Lofts Lofts Lofts Lofts Lofts Lofts Lofts Lofts Lofts Lofts Lofts Lofts Lofts Lofts L

ofts Lofts Lofts Lofts Lofts Lofts Lofts Lofts Lofts Lofts Lofts Lofts Lofts Lofts Lofts Lofts Lofts Lof

Living Working **Shopping** Living Working Shopping Living **Working** Shopping **Living** Working Shopping I

g Living **Working** Shopping **Living** Working **Shopping** Living **Working** Shopping **Living** Working **Shopping**

Working **Shopping** Living Working Shopping Living **Working** Shopping **Living** Working Shopping Living W

The loft is an American creation, from the beginning of the 1940s, which started with the conversion of warehouses and factories to create homes or work spaces. The majority of the loft buildings in New York were constructed at the end of the 19th century and the beginning of the 20th century, for small manufacturing businesses.

In the 1930s and 1940s, New York's manufacturing industry moved to larger complexes outside the city, leaving textile factories, printers, upholsterers, laundries, warehouses and production premises in disuse. The previously prosperous financial district of Soho was abandoned as businesses moved to Wall Street and Greenwich Village, and it became the perfect environment for artists who were looking for large spaces with low rents.

AMERICAN ORIGINS

The infrastructures of the first lofts barely met the basic needs for habitation, and constituted a new form of clandestine life. Lofts represented the defense of architecture which had been declared obsolete by the industrial sector, and they soon came to represent a life-style in which art formed part of every day living. Little by little, this atmosphere created a way of life which was based on the underground *avant-garde* culture of the 1950s.

In the 1970s this cultural movement gave way to the installation of businesses such as restaurants, shops and galleries, and by the end of the 1990s Soho had become a constant focal point which generated trends in fashion, art and design.

Der *Loft* ist eine amerikanische Idee aus den Anfängen
der 1940er Jahre, entstanden aus der Umwandlung von
Lagerhallen und Fabriken in Wohn- oder Arbeitsräume.
Die Großzahl der *Loft*-Gebäude in New York entstand
Ende des 19., Anfang des 20. Jahrhunderts im Sektor
der Leichtindustrie und Manufakturen.
In den 1930er und 40er Jahren wurden die New Yorker
Manufakturen in größere, außerhalb der Stadt gelegene
Gebäude verlagert. Daraufhin standen zahlreiche der
Textilfabriken, Druckereien, Lagerhallen, Polstereien,
Wäschereien und andere Produktionsstätten komplett leer.
Das einst wohlhabende Viertel Soho, nun verlassen und
trostlos – die neuen Zentren befanden sich an der Wall
Street und Greenwich Village –, fand schnell neue
Bewohner: Künstler, die große Räumlichkeiten zu
günstigen Mieten benötigten.

DIE AMERIKANISCHE HERKUNFT

Die Ausstattung der ersten *Lofts* genügte kaum den täglichen Anforderungen, es wurde jedoch mit ihnen eine neue, unkonventionelle Lebensform geschaffen. Ihre Bewohner wurden zu Aktivisten – diese belebten eine Architektur wieder, die von der Industrie als überflüssig erklärt worden war, und repräsentierten eine neue Lebensform, in der die Kunst sich mit dem Alltag vermischte: die Avantgarde, der Underground der 50er Jahre.

Bereits in den 70er Jahren wurde diese Bewegung von Restaurants, Geschäften und Galerien aus den Lofts verdrängt. Bis Ende der 90er Jahre sollte sich Soho in ein Viertel entwickelt haben, in dem stets die neuesten Tendenzen von Mode, Kunst und Design ihren Anfang finden.

Le loft est une invention américaine issue de la reconversion, au début des années 1940, d'entrepôts et d'usines en lieux d'habitation ou de travail. À New York, la plupart des édifices transformés ont été construits à la fin du XIXe siècle et au début du XXe siècle pour le compte de l'industrie légère et manufacturière.

Au cours des années 1930 et 1940, les industriels new-yorkais ont déserté le quartier de Soho pour s'installer dans des complexes industriels plus spacieux à la périphérie de la ville. Entrepôts, filatures, halles et usines sont peu à peu laissés à l'abandon. Ce district financier autrefois prospère se retrouva isolé du nouveau centre, désormais situé autour de Wall Street et de Greenwich Village. Les espaces délaissés furent loués ou achetés à bas prix par des artistes, qui les transformèrent pour y vivre et travailler.

LE MODÈLE AMÉRICAIN

Mais les infrastructures de ces premiers ateliers satisfaisaient à peine aux exigences d'habitabilité élémentaires et correspondaient à un mode de vie marginal. Investis par d'ardents défenseurs d'une architecture que le secteur industriel avait déclaré obsolète, ils furent bientôt représentatifs d'un style de vie où l'art participait du quotidien. Il se dégagea peu à peu de ce climat un style et une esthétique de vie qui prirent corps au sein de l'avant-garde *underground* des années 1950. Le loft était né.

Dans les années 1970, ce mouvement culturel laissa place à l'implantation de commerces, tels que restaurants, boutiques et galeries. Et vers la fin des années 1990, le quartier de Soho devint le point de référence et le creuset des dernières tendances en matière de mode, d'art et de design.

De loft is een Amerikaanse creatie van circa 1940, die ontstond door de transformatie van pakhuizen en fabrieken tot woningen of kantoren. De meeste gebouwen met lofts in New York zijn eind 19e eeuw en begin 20e eeuw gebouwd als fabrieken en hallen voor de lichte industrie. Rond 1930 en 1940 weken New Yorkse fabrikanten uit naar grotere complexen buiten de stad, waardoor textielfabrieken, drukkerijen, pakhuizen, stoffeerderijen, wasserijen en productiehallen leeg kwamen te staan. Het voorheen welvarende financiële district Soho werd verlaten toen de handel zich verplaatste naar Wall Street en Greenwich Village. Soho bleek een bij uitstek geschikte plek voor kunstenaars op zoek naar grote ateliers met lage huren.

VAN AMERIKAANSE ORIGINE

De eerste lofts konden maar nauwelijks voldoen aan de basale wooneisen en werden vaak clandestien bewoond. Ze vertegenwoordigden de felle verdediging van een door de industriële sector afgeschreven architectuur en stonden al snel voor een levensstijl waarin kunst deel uitmaakte van het dagelijks leven. Geleidelijk ontstonden er uit deze sfeer een leefstijl en esthetiek gebaseerd op de avant-gardistische cultuur van de underground van de jaren vijftig.

Al in de jaren zeventig maakte deze culturele beweging plaats voor bepaalde vormen van handel, zoals restaurants, winkels en galerieën. Omstreek 2000 was Soho veranderd in de plek waar trends onstonden op het gebied van mode, kunst en design.

In the Europe, the use of lofts for homes, offices and commercial premises started in London.
Following their resounding success in the United States in the 1970s and 1980s, lofts became places for artistic production, but were also evocative, psychologically active spaces where the owner could express himself with freedom and feel complete.
In London and in Paris, living in a loft was considered an eccentricity reserved for the rich and creative, and represented a personal choice rather than a mass movement.
The conversion of the old Bryant & May match factory in London in the 1980s (a project which was later developed by London Buildings) was presented as 'a New York-style loft in East London'. The project offered the public

EUROPEAN TRENDS

apartments equipped with the essentials and, although less basic than the originals in New York, they proved very popular. Consequently, London Buildings went on to convert other industrial properties into lofts for residential use.

In Berlin, the conversion of factories and warehouses to create spaces to live and work was marked by the squatter movement, and those who became known as the 'loft people'. Both movements took advantage of the huge number of abandoned apartments in renovated areas, creating a new cultural and social space in a city divided by the wall.

Another example of converting buildings is marked by the experience of Groningen in Holland, where harbor warehouses were transformed into lofts for students.

In Europa war London die Stadt, in der die ersten *Lofts* als Wohn-, Arbeits- und Geschäftsräume dienten. Aufgrund ihres großen Erfolgs in den USA waren *Lofts* in den 70er und 80er Jahren in London vor allem bei Künstlern beliebt. Sie galten als inspirierende Orte, an denen man sich frei entfalten konnte.

Von London bis Paris waren *Lofts* jedoch für besonders wohlhabende und kreative Menschen reserviert und wurden daher nie zum Massenphänomen.

Die Umwandlung der alten Phosphorfabrik Bryant & May in London in den 80er Jahren (ein von London Buildings entwickeltes Projekt) wurde als „*Loft* im New Yorker Stil im Osten von London" präsentiert. In diesem Projekt wurden Wohnungen geschaffen, die man nur mit dem Nötigsten

LOFTS IN EUROPA

ausstattete – trotz der Tatsache, dass sie viel raffinierter als ihre Vorbilder in New York waren, fanden sie viel Anklang. Aufgrund des Erfolgs wandelte London Buildings noch weitere Industriegebäude in bewohnbare *Lofts* um. In Berlin fand die Umwandlung von Fabriken und Lagerhallen in Wohn- und Arbeitsräume einerseits in der Besetzerszene, andererseits bei den sogenannten *Loft People* ihren Anfang. Beide Bewegungen profitierten von der riesigen Anzahl verlassener Gebäuden und schufen somit in der geteilten Stadt neue kulturelle und soziale Räume.
Ein anderes Beispiel für eine sinnvolle Nutzung solcher Gebäude ist Groningen in den Niederlanden, wo Lagerhallen am Hafen in *Loft* für Studenten umgewandelt wurden.

En Europe, c'est à Londres que naît le phénomène du loft conçu comme un lieu d'habitation, de travail et de commerce. Profitant de l'engouement suscité aux États-Unis durant les années 1970 et 1980, les lofts n'y sont plus seulement des lieux de création artistique et y jouent le rôle d'espaces séduisants, doués d'une âme, où le propriétaire des lieux peut s'exprimer librement et se réaliser.

À Londres comme à Paris, habiter un loft est alors atypique, et semble réservé aux artistes et aux créateurs aisés : il s'agit davantage d'afficher un style de vie différent du commun des mortels, qui combine un espace de travail idéal et un lieu de vie parfait.

Dans les années 1980, la reconversion de l'ancienne usine d'allumettes Bryant & May, à Londres (un projet que développera plus tard London Buildings) est présenté comme « le loft de style new-yorkais de l'est londonien ».

LE STYLE EUROPÉEN

Ce projet offre au public des appartements tout équipés qui rencontrent un grand succès en dépit d'un raffinement bien supérieur à leurs homologues new-yorkais. London Buildings se chargera ensuite de reconvertir d'autres bâtiments industriels en loft résidentiels.

À Berlin, la transformation d'usines et d'entrepôts en espaces où vivre et travailler est avant tout le fait des squatters et de ce qu'il est convenu d'appeler les *loft people,* deux mouvements qui sauront tirer parti de l'énorme quantité d'appartements abandonnés, et créeront un nouvel espace culturel et social dans les quartiers rénovés de la ville divisée par le mur.

La remarquable expérience de Groningen, aux Pays-Bas, est un autre exemple de reconversion réussie, avec la transformation d'entrepôts portuaires en lofts pour étudiants.

In Europa begon de opkomst van lofts als plek om te wonen, te werken en handel te drijven in Londen. Voortbordurend op het enorme succes in de VS tussen 1970 en 1990 werden de lofts naast plekken voor artistieke productie ook suggestieve, psychologisch actieve ruimten, waarin de eigenaar zich in vrijheid kon uitdrukken en ontplooien.

Zowel in Parijs als in Londen werd het wonen in een loft gezien als een excentriciteit die was voorbehouden aan de rijken en creatieven, en stond het meer voor een individuele keuze dan voor een algemene trend.

De transformatie van de oude luciferfabriek Bryant & May in Londen in de jaren tachtig (een project dat daarna werd ontwikkeld door Londen Buildings) werd gepresenteerd als een 'loft in New Yorkse stijl in Oost-Londen'. Dit project bood het publiek met het hoognodige uitgeruste

DE EUROPESE TENDENS

appartementen die, hoewel ze veel verfijnder waren dan de New Yorkse lofts, gretig aftrek vonden. Op dezelfde manier nam Londen Buildings de verbouwing van andere industriële gebouwen en ruimten tot woonplekken voor zijn rekening.

In Berlijn werd de verandering van fabrieken en pakhuizen in plekken om te wonen en te werken gemarkeerd door de krakersbeweging, okupa, ook wel bekend als de loft people. De krakers benutten de enorme hoeveelheid gebouwen in verlaten wijken en creëerden een nieuwe culturele en sociale ruimte in de door een muur verdeelde stad.

Een ander voorbeeld van de verandering van gebouwen vormt de waardevolle ervaring in Groningen, Nederland, waar scheepspakhuizen werden omgebouwd tot studentenwoningen.

MOULIN ROUGE
BAL
DU
LIN ROUGE
Féerie
Féerie
LA REVUE DU MOULIN ROUGE

LIVING

RESIDENCE IN TORONTO

Cecconi Simone

Toronto, Canada

© Joy von Tiederman

FOUR-LEVEL LOFT

Joan Bach

Barcelona, Spain

© Jordi Miralles

RENAUD RESIDENCE

Cha & Innerhofer Architecture & Design
New York, United States

© Dao Lou Zha

MICHIGAN AVENUE APARTMENT

Pablo Uribe

Miami, United States

© Pep Escoda

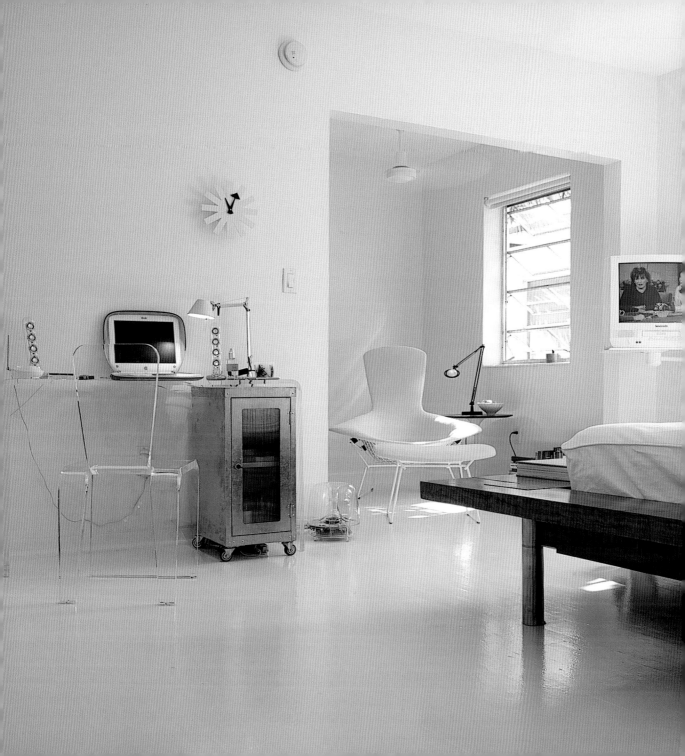

SMITH APARTMENT

Smart Design Studio

Sydney, Australia

© Sharrin Rees

SPATIAL RELATIONS

McDonnell Associates

London, United Kingdom

© Carlos Domínguez

A CONTINUAL PATH

Luis Cuartas & Guillermo Arias

Bogotá, Colombia

© Eduardo Consuegra

APARTMENT IN MILAN

Luca Rolla

Milan, Italy

© Andrea Martiradonna

AROUND TABLE

Smart Architects

Sydney, Australia

© Gene Raymond Ross

APARTMENT IN LISBON

Inês Lobo

Lisbon, Portugal

© Sergio Mah

LA MAGDALENA APARTMENT

Guillermo Arias

Bogotá, Colombia

© Pablo Rojas & Álvaro Gutiérrez

SMITH LOFT

Cho Slade Architects

New York, United States

© Jordi Miralles

LOFT A

Carlo Donati

Milan, Italy

© Matteo Piazza

ATRIUM LOFT

Nancy Robbins & Blau-Centre de la Llar

Barcelona, Spain

© José Luis Hausmann

CAMPINS LOFT

Luis Felipe Infiesta

Barcelona, Spain

© Jordi Sarrà

MAURO LOFT

The owner

Barcelona, Spain

© Jordi Sarrà

RUE VOLTA LOFT

Christophe Ponceau

Paris, France

© Alejandro Bahamón

BROWN LOFT

Deborah Berke

New York, United States

© Catherine Tighe

INSPIRED BY ICE

Marie Veronique de Hoop Scheffer

Buenos Aires, Argentina

© Virginia del Giúdice

DECORATOR'S LOFT

Dorotea Oliva

Buenos Aires, Argentina

© Virginia del Giúdice

STEWART LOFT

James Gauer

New York, United States

© Catherine Tighe

FORMAL UNITY

Guillermo Arias

Bogotá, Colombia

© Eduardo Consuegra, Pablo Rojas

UNIQUE SQUARE LOFT

James Dart

New York, United States

© Catherine Tighe

RECTANGULAR LOFT

Pablo Chiaporri

Buenos Aires, Argentina

© Virginia del Giúdice

FOUR ATMOSPHERE IN ONE

Hugh Broughton Architects

Gloucestershire, United Kingdom

© Carlos Domínguez

CHOIR LOFT

Delson or Sherman Architects

New York, United States

© Catherine Tighe

WAGNER LOFT

Michael Carapetian

Venice, Italy

© Andrea Martiradonna

ONE SPACE INSIDE ANOTHER

Alexander Jiménez

New York, United States

PARK AVENUE LOFT

Ayhan Ozan Architects

New York, United States

© Björg Photography

SPACE FOR TWO

Guillermo Arias

Cartagena de Indias, Colombia

© Carlos Tobón

HORIZONTAL UNIT

Stephen Quinn & Elise Ovanessoff

London, United Kingdom

© Jordi Miralles

TWO ATMOSPHERE AND ONE BOX

Mónica Pla

Barcelona, Spain

© José Luis Hausmann

LOFT WITHIN A LOFT

Studio A

Milan, Italy

© Andrea Martiradonna

STRUCTURAL LOFT

Attilio Stocchi

Bergamo, Italy

© Andrea Martiradonna

HOME AND ATELIER

Luis Benedit

Buenos Aires, Argentina

© Virginia del Giúdice

HOME AND ATELIER II

Pablo Chiaporri

Buenos Aires, Argentina

© Virginia del Giúdice

PAINTER'S STUDIO

Agnès Blanch/Elina Vila (Minim Arquitectura Interior)

Barcelona, Spain

© José Luis Hausmann

LOFT IN CHELSEA

Kar-Hwa Ho

New York, United States

© Björg Photography

LOFT IN PLAZA MAYOR

Manuel Ocaña del Valle

Madrid, Spain

© Alfonso Postigo

LOFT IN SÃO PAULO

Brunete Fraccaroli
São Paulo, Brasil

© João Ribeiro

RESIDENCE IN SURRY HILLS

Smart Design Studio
New South Wales, Australia

© Sharrin Rees

RP APARTMENT

Daniele Geltrudi

Busto Arsizio, Italy

© Andrea Martiradonna

TOP-RECOLETA RENTAL

Mariana Bischof

Buenos Aires, Argentina

© Germán Falke

LOFT IN CIUTAT VELLA

M. Vives, Ll. Escarmis/GCA Arquitectes

Barcelona, Spain

© Jordi Miralles

LOFT IN TEL AVIV

Alex Meitlis

Tel Aviv, Israel

© Yael Pincus

LOFT IN MELBOURNE

Six Degrees Architects

Melbourne, Australia

© Shania Shegedyn

LOFT FLATIRON

Slade Architecture

New York, United States

© Jordi Miralles

LOFT IN GRÀCIA

Joan Bach, Jordi Viladomiu, Ignaci Mas
Barcelona, Spain

© Jordi Miralles

LOFT ON UNDERWOOD STREET

Hugh Broughton Architects
London, United Kingdom

© Carlos Domínguez

STYLE DESIGNER

Non Kicht Group

Bruges, Belgium

© Jan Verlinde

ART AND HUMOR

Orefelt Associates

London, United Kingdom

© Alberto Ferrero

GOOD NEWS AND BAD NEWS: A man walked into a doctor's office to get a check-up. After the examination the doctor says to the man, I've got good news and I've got bad news. The bad news is your going to die in a year and there's nothing you can do about it. The good news is I'm having an affair with my secretary.

BW2 LOFT

AG & F Architetti

Brescia, Italy

© Andrea Martiradonna

DOBINSKY LOFT

Eyal Dobinsky

Tel Aviv, Israel

© Yael Pincus

LOFT ON AVENUE PHILIPPE AUGUSTE

Studio Maréchaux Architectes

Paris, France

© Pascal Maréchaux

LOFT IN BELLEVILLE

Bernard Gory

Paris, France

© Christian Zachariassen

BROOME LOFT

Moneo Brock

Paris, France

© Jordi Miralles

LOFT IN POBLE NOU

Sandra Aparicio i Forteza Carbonell Associats
Barcelona, Spain

© Santiago Garcés

LOFT IN IVRY SUR SEINE

Laurence Vittet-Lecluyse, François Lemasne

Ivry sur Seine, France

© Berto Lecluyse

HUNTER RITACO LOFT

Ruhl Walker Architects

Boston, United States

© Jordi Miralles

LOFT ON RUE DE PYRÉNÉES

Stéphane Zamfirescu

Paris, France

© Olivier Hallot and Jacques Giaume

LOFT PARIS 100ÈME

Philippe Demougeot

Paris, France

© Daniel Moulinet

LOFT ON RUE HUYGHENS

Studio Maréchaux Architectes

Paris, France

© Pascal Maréchaux

WORKING

MINDFIELD

Shubin & Donalson Architects

Marina del Rey, California

© Tom Bonner Photography

OGILVY & MATTHER

Shubin & Donalson Architects, Eric Owen Moss

Los Angeles, United States

© Tom Bonner Photography

SOCIEDAD GENERAL DE AUTORES

Rafael Cáceres Zurita

Barcelona, Spain

© Jordi Miralles

IWIN.COM

Shubin & Donaldson Architects

Los Angeles, United States

© Tom Bonner Photography

MK/3-VA

Sarah Bitter/Metek Architecture

Paris, France

© Pep Escoda

Fondation Maeght   3 juillet - 5 novembre 2002   Henry Moore
06570 Saint-Paul

GOLDEN NUGGET

INNOCAD Planung und Projektmanagement

Graz, Austria

© Pep Escoda

RIOS CLEMENTI HALE STUDIOS OFFICE

Rios Clementi Hale Studio

Los Angeles, United States

The California Endowment

STUDIO DATRANS

Chen Xudong, Shen Yirong, Gu Jirong/Datrans
Shangai, China

© Datrans

HYDRAULX

Shubin & Donaldson Architects

Santa Monica, United States

© Tom Bonner Photography

DDB OFFICE HONG KONG

CL3 Architects

Hong Kong, China

© CL3 Architects

GROUND ZERO ADVERTISING

Shubin & Donaldson Architects

Marina del Rey, California

© Tom Bonner Photography

PINCELLI

Domenico Biondi/Progettisti Associati

Sassuolo, Italy

© Matteo Piazza

CADOR HEADQUARTERS

Cador

Madrid, Spain

© Jordi Miralles

CENTRO GESTOR

Salvador Giné

Lleida, Spain

© Jordi Miralles

DALTON'S DIGITAL BROTHERS

Mariano Martín Domínguez
Madrid, Spain

© Eduardo Sánchez López

WORKSHIP STREET

Jestico & Whiles

London, United Kingdom

© Jestico & Whiles

CLOUD 9

Enric Ruiz, Olga Subirós/Cloud 9

Barcelona, Spain

© Luis Ros

DWELLING FOR AN EXECUTIVE

Brunete Fraccaroli

São Paulo, Brasil

© Tuca Reinés

WEDDING LOFT

Brunete Fraccaroli

Berlin, Germany

© Hendrik Blaukat

LOFT IN ABBOT KINNEY

Mark Mack Architects

Venice, Italy

© Undine Pröhl

ATTIC IN BILBAO

AV62 Arquitectos

Bilbao, Spain

© Susana Aréchaga + Luis Ambrós

CHRISTOPHE PILLET APARTMENT

Christophe Pillet

Paris, France

© Omnia

LOFT ON RUE DE TUNIS

Guilhem Roustan

Paris, France

© Daniel Moulinet

RESIDENTIAL LABORATORY

Petersen & Verwers

San Francisco, United States

© Marion Brenner

LOFT CORTINES

Joan Bach

Barcelona, Spain

© Jordi Miralles

LOFT SERT

Heres Arquitectura

Barcelona, Spain

© Jordi Miralles

SHOPPING

HARE BUCHWEAR

OUT.DeSIGN

Kyoto, Japan

© Kozo Takayama

LA CENTRAL DEL RAVAL

Enric Granell

Barcelona, Spain

© Alejandro Bachrach

IN MAT. ARTQUITECT

José Luis López Ibáñez

Barcelona, Spain

© Joan Mundó

el guiño la despedida, ¿por qué no un fina...
el sueño llega a su fin, y el objeto se des...
en forma de luz.

HARE BUCHWEAR

OUT.DeSIGN

Kyoto, Japan

© Kozo Takayama

pineau

SPAZIONAVIGLI

Roberto Brambilla & Associates

New York, United States

© Jordi Miralles

PATINA

Belzberg Architects

Los Angeles, United States

© Tom Bonner Photography

FALCON

John Friedman & Alice Kimm Architects

Los Angeles, United States

© Benny Chan/Fotoworks

SITA MURT

Bailo & Rull Arquitectura

Manresa, Spain

© Jordi Miralles

ADAM ET ROPÉ FEMME/HOMME

OUT.DeSIGN

Kyoto, Japan

© Kozo Takayama

B-JIRUSHI YOSHIDA

Wonder Wall

Gaikanyama, Japan

© Kozo Takayama

14 ONCE

Studio 63

Florence, Italy

© Yael Pincus

AMARCORD

Guillermo Blanco

Madrid, Spain

© Rodrigo Pérez

ADAM ET ROPÉ FEMME/HOMME SENDAI

OUT.DeSIGN

Sendai, Japan

© Kozo Takayama

EAST HOTEL BAR

Jordan Mozer & Associates

Hamburg, Germany

© Designhotels.com

CLAN CAFÉ

LAI – Laboratorio Architettura Interni
Milan, Italy

© Andrea Martiradonna

MYKITA

Mykita

Berlin, Germany

© Mykita

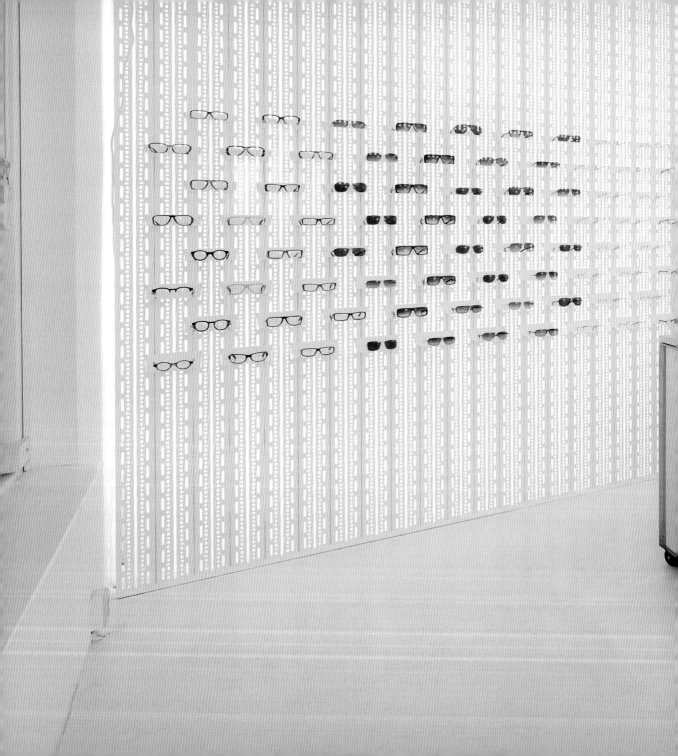

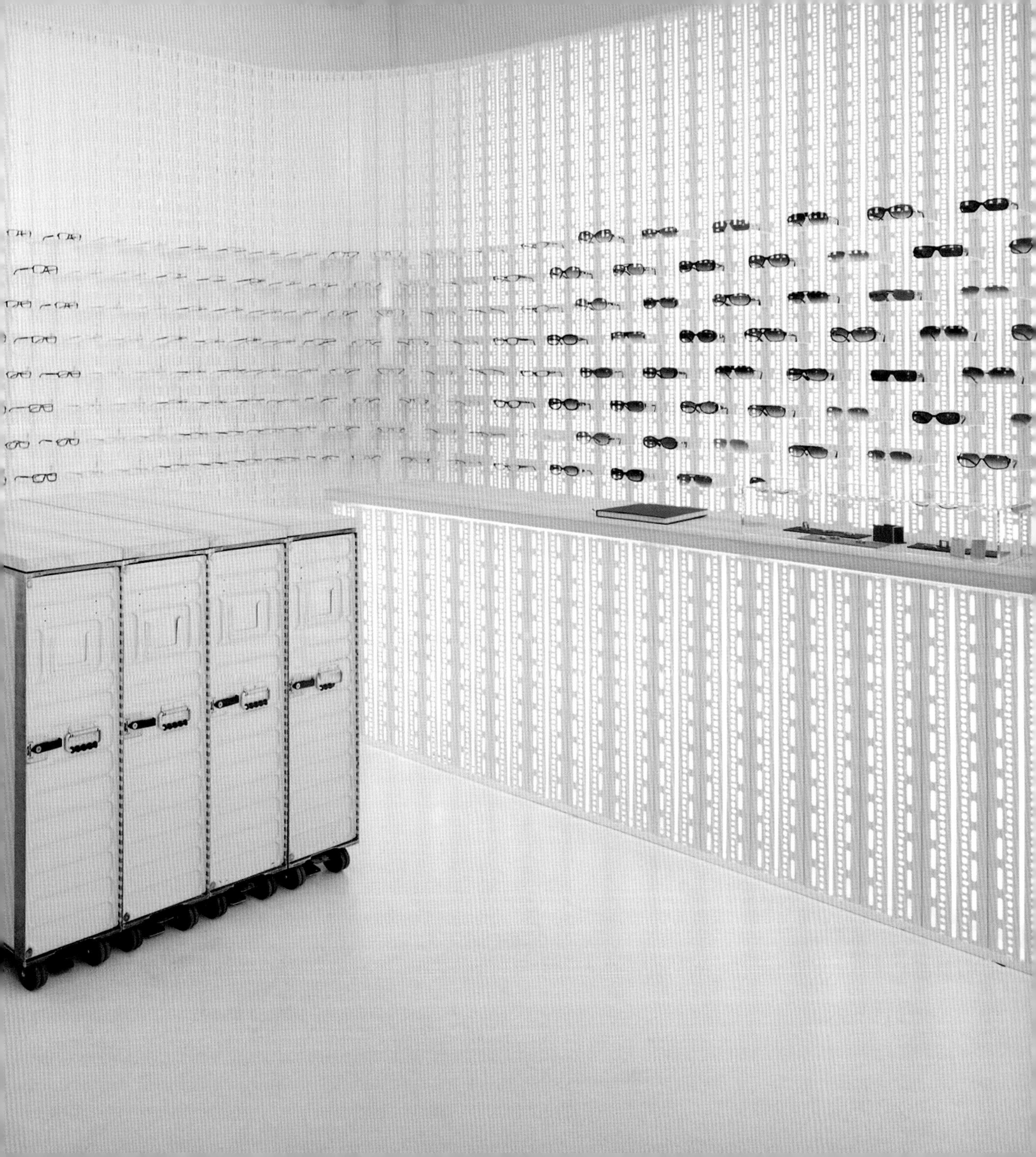

NATURA

Arthur Casas Arquitectura e Design

Paris, France

© Tuca Reinés

ENERGY LONDON

Studio 63

London, United Kingdom

© Yael Pincus

KOSUSHI

Arthur Casas Arquitectura e Design

São Paulo, Brasil

© Tuca Reinés

KARMA

Rajiv Saini Associates

Bombay, India

© Courtesy RS+A

MAGAZZINI SERMONETA SHOP

Duccio Grassi Architects

Reggio Emilia, Rome, Italy

© Andrea Martiradonna

MANNER

BEHF

Vienna, Austria

© Rupert Steiner

SHOP GRAZ

EOK – Eichinger Oder Knechtl

Vienna, Austria

© Rupert Steiner

BAR VELOCE

AC2 Studio

New York, United States

© Michael Moran

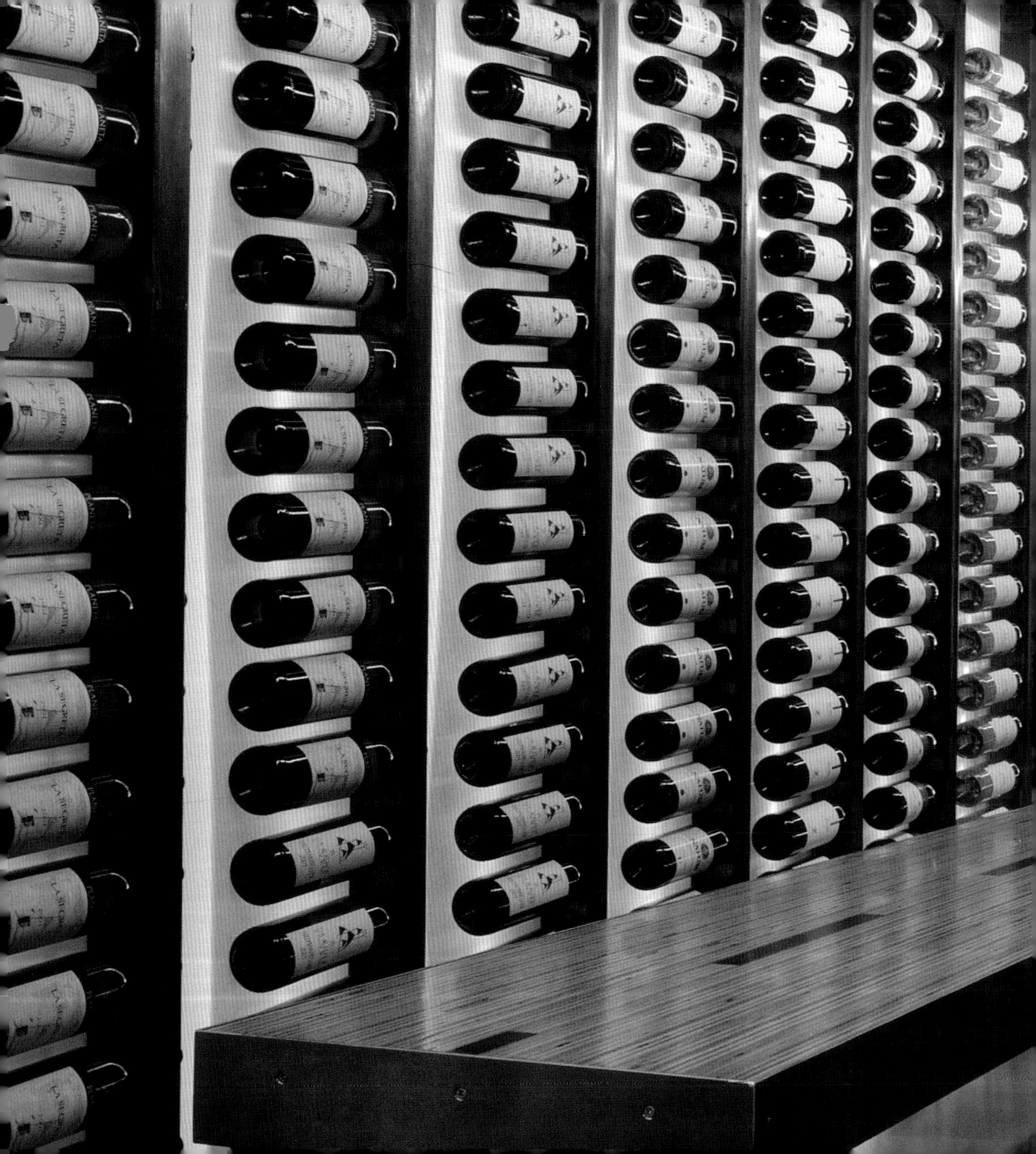

CAFÉ HUDSON

Philippe Stark

New York, United States

© Jordi Miralles

FABBRICA

Tjep.

Rotterdam, The Netherlands

© Daniel Nicolas, Tjep.

ZOOM-IN

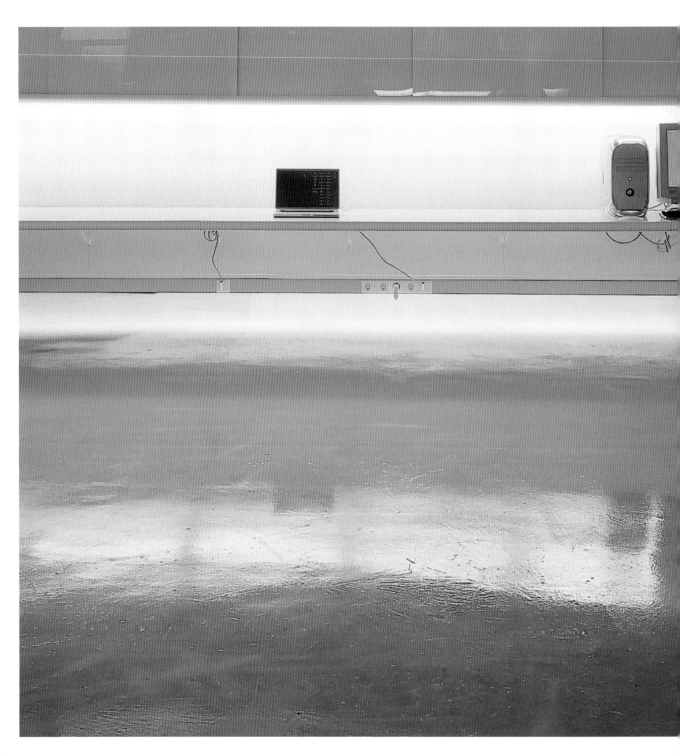